RIDICULOUS NICHOLAS RIDDLE BOOK

by Joseph Rosenbloom
drawings by Joyce Behr

Sterling Publishing Co., Inc.   New York

In this series
Ridiculous Nicholas Pet Riddle Book

Library of Congress Cataloging in Publication Data

Rosenbloom, Joseph.
  Ridiculous Nicholas riddle book.
  Includes index.
  Summary: Drawings and text consisting solely
of riddles follow a boy through his daily activities
from the time he wakes up until he turns in for
the night.
  1. Riddles, Juvenile. [1. Riddles] I. Behr,
Joyce, ill. II. Title.
PN6371.5.R613   818'.5402   81-50988
ISBN 0-8069-4652-0   AACR2
ISBN 0-8069-4653-9 (lib. bdg.)

Oak Tree 7061-2816-8

Text copyright © 1981 by Joseph Rosenbloom,
illustrations copyright © 1981 by Joyce Behr
Published by Sterling Publishing Co., Inc.
Two Park Avenue, New York, N.Y. 10016
Distributed in Australia by Oak Tree Press Co., Ltd.
P.O. Box J34, Brickfield Hill, Sydney 2000, N.S.W.
Distributed in the United Kingdom by Oak Tree Press Ltd. U.K.
Available in Canada from Oak Tree Press Ltd.
℅ Canadian Manda Group, 215 Lakeshore Boulevard East
Toronto, Ontario M5A 3W9
Manufactured in the United States of America
All rights reserved

Why did Nicholas put
the banana peel next
to his bed?

So he could slip
out of bed in
the morning.

Why did Nicholas hit the clock?

Because the clock
struck first.

What did the sock say to Nicholas?

"You're putting me on!"

Why did Nicholas
take his comb
to the dentist?

Because it lost a tooth.

Why did Zelda
shut her eyes
in the kitchen?

So she wouldn't see the
orange peel and the bacon strip.

What two things
can't Nicholas
have for breakfast?

Lunch and
dinner.

Why did Nicholas throw the
butter out of the window?

He wanted to see
the butterfly.

Why didn't Nicholas
take the bus
to school?

It wouldn't fit through the door.

When is a kindergarten teacher like a squirrel?

When she is surrounded by a bunch of little nuts.

What is black when it is clean and white when it is dirty?

A blackboard.

Why did Nicholas stand on his head?

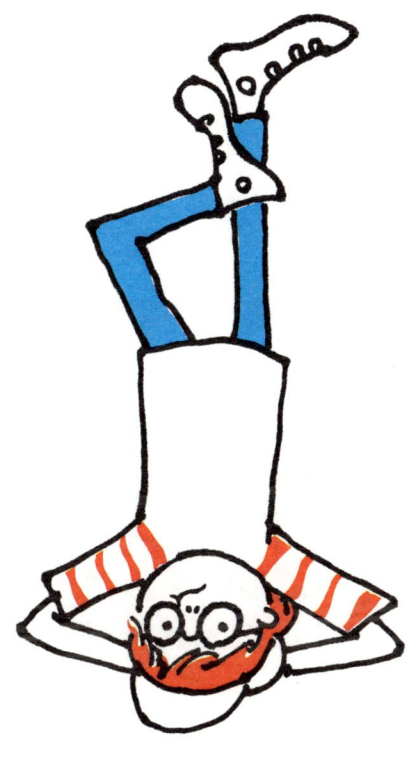

He was trying
to turn things over
in his mind.

What kind of table

has no legs?

A multiplication table.

Why don't mice like arithmetic?

Because if you add 4 + 4 . . .

you get ate.

How do you divide five apples among three people?

Make apple sauce.

What do you get
if you add
5Q and 5Q?

10Q.

You're welcome!

How many sides
does a box have?

Two. The inside and the outside.

Why did Zelda
put lipstick on
her forehead?

She was trying
to make up
her mind.

What fruit do
we find in
history?

Dates.

Why did Nicholas
eat the
dollar bill?

Because it was his lunch money.